Flower ABC Coloring Book

Flower ABC Coloring Book

Nina Barbaresi

Dover Publications, Inc.
New York

Published in Canada by General Publishing Company, Ltd., 30 Lesmill Road, Don Mills, Toronto, Ontario.

Published in the United Kingdom by Constable and Company, Ltd., 3 The Lanchesters, 162–164 Fulham Palace Road, London W6 9ER.

Flower ABC Coloring Book is a new work, first published by Dover Publications, Inc., in 1992.

International Standard Book Number: 0-486-27309-1

Manufactured in the United States of America
Dover Publications, Inc., 31 East 2nd Street, Mineola, N.Y. 11501

Publisher's Note

A is for Aster and Z is for Zinnia! These pretty flowers, plus daffodils, roses, tulips, lilies and lots more, will make learning lots of fun. All 26 letters of the alphabet are pictured for you to color with crayons or pencils. Right next to each letter is a picture of a flower beginning with that letter. Now you can learn the alphabet—and the names of lots of flowers—as you color your very own garden.

Flower ABC Coloring Book

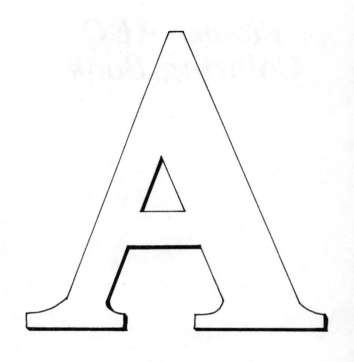

Aster

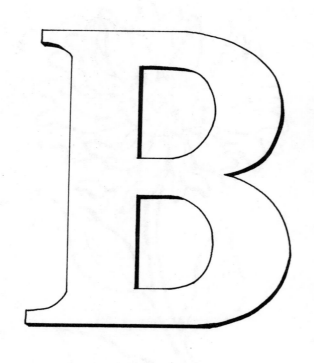

Buttercup

13

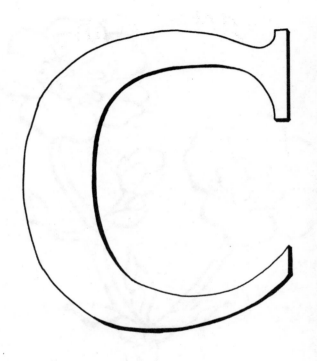

Carnation

15

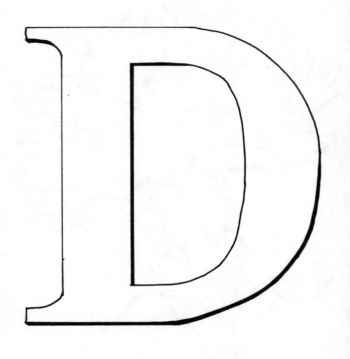

Daffodil

17

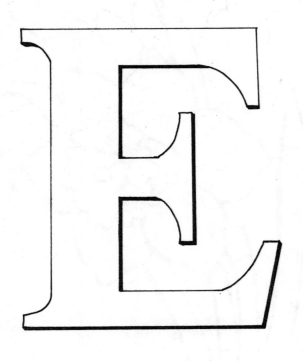

Edelweiss

19

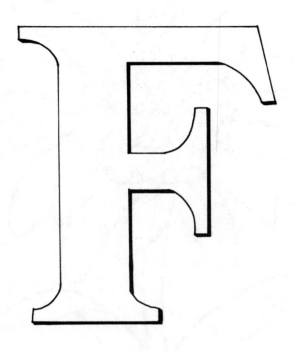

Foxglove

21

Geranium

23

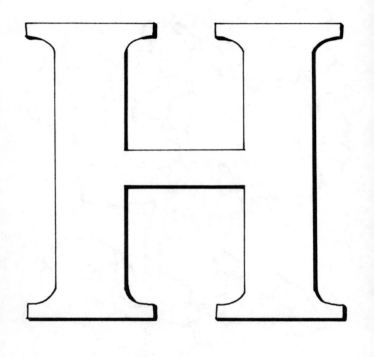

Hollyhock

25

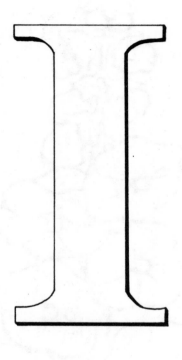

Iris

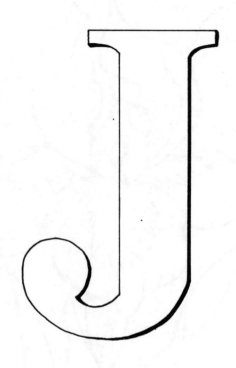

Jack-in-the-Pulpit

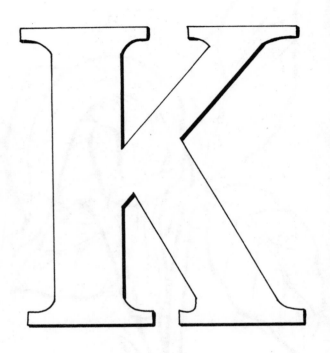

Kalanchoe

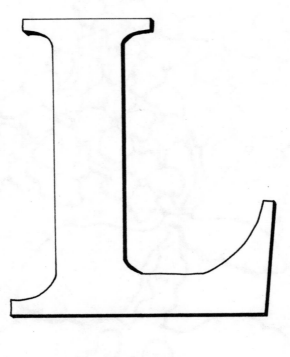

Lily

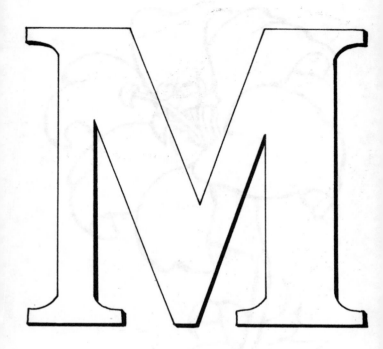

Morning Glory

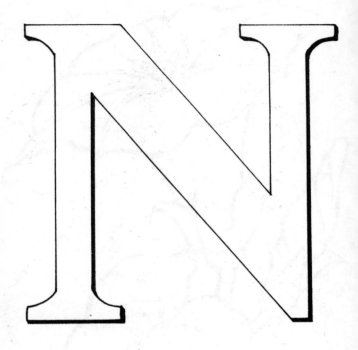

Nasturtium

37

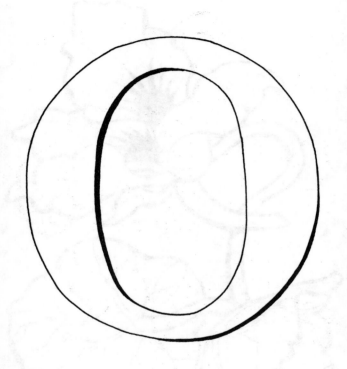

Orchid

39

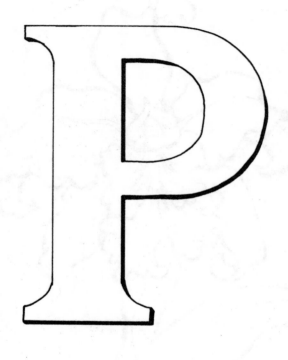

Pansy

41

Queen Anne's Lace

43

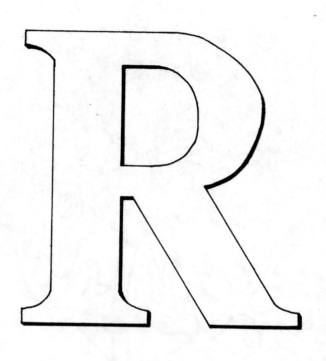

Rose

45

Snapdragon

47

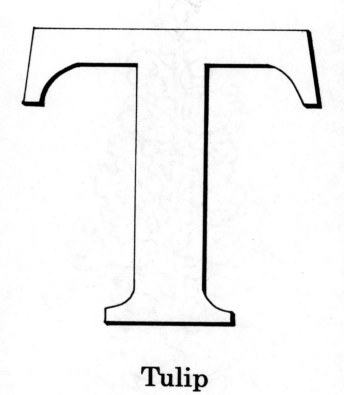

Tulip

Umbrella Tree

Violet

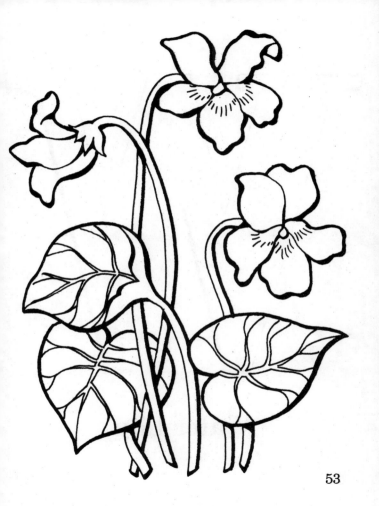

53

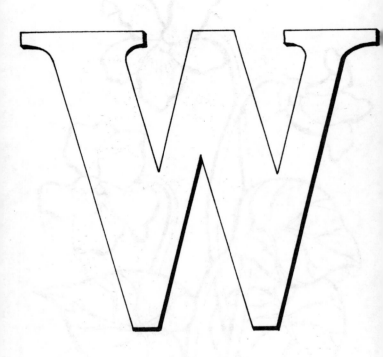

Water Lily

Xanthia

Yarrow

Zinnia

61